A106 09/09

APR 1 4 2006

D0579410

WITHDRAWN

LIVING WELL

SAFETY IN
PUBLIC PLACES

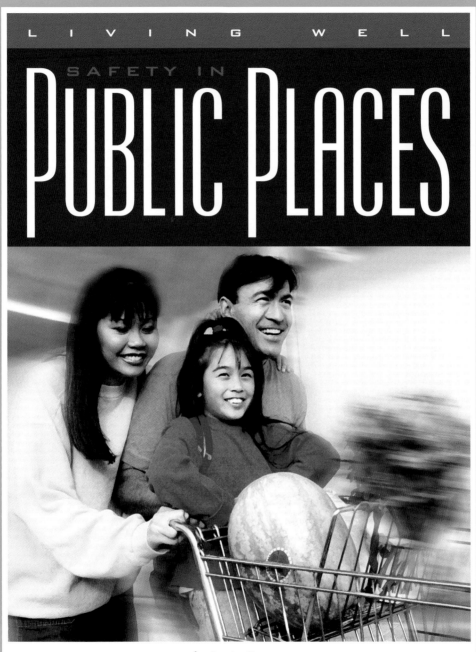

by Lucia Raatma

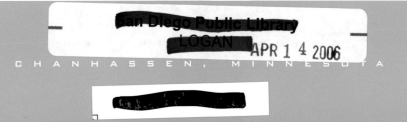

San Diego Public Library
LOGAN   APR 1 4 2006

C H A N H A S S E N ,   M I N N E S O T A

Published in the United States of America by The Child's World®
PO Box 326, Chanhassen, MN 55317-0326
800-599-READ
www.childsworld.com

Content Adviser:
Bridget Clementi,
Safe Kids Coordinator,
Children's Health
Education Center,
Milwaukee, Wisconsin

Photo Credits: Cover/frontispiece: Corbis; cover corner: Getty Images/Photodisc/Nancy R. Cohen. Interior: Corbis: 8 (Michael Keller), 14 (Morton Beebe), 18 (Bill Varie), 25 (David H. Wells), 26 (Ronnie Kaufman); Getty Images/The Image Bank: 10 (Alain Daussin), 21 (Steve Taylor); Getty Images/Photodisc: 19 (Alexander Walter), 20; Getty Images/Stone: 5 (Dennis Kitchen), 11 (Tom Schierlitz), 12 (Anthony Marsland), 13 (Don Smetzer), 31 (Robert E. Daemmrich); PictureQuest: 17 (Frederic Cirou/PhotoAlto), 22 (Ron Chapple/Thinkstock), 23 (Nancy Pierce/Black Star Publishing), 27 (Digital Vision); Stock, Boston Inc./PictureQuest: 6 (David C. Binder) 15 (Bob Daemmrich); David Young-Wolff/PhotoEdit: 16, 24.

The Child's World®: Mary Berendes, Publishing Director

Editorial Directions, Inc.: E. Russell Primm, Editorial Director; Katie Marsico, Line Editor; Matt Messbarger, Editorial Assistant; Susan Hindman, Copy Editor; Sarah E. De Capua, Proofreader; Katherine Trickle and Stephen Carl Wender, Fact Checkers; Tim Griffin/IndexServ, Indexer; Cian Loughlin O'Day, Photo Researcher; Linda S. Koutris, Photo Selector

The Design Lab: Kathleen Petelinsek, Design; Kari Thornborough, Page Production

Copyright © 2005 by The Child's World®
All rights reserved. No part of this book may be reproduced or utilized in
any form or by any means without written permission from the publisher.

Library of Congress Cataloging-in-Publication Data
Raatma, Lucia.
  Safety in public places / by Lucia Raatma.
    v. cm. — (Living well)
Includes bibliographical references and index.
  Contents: At the amusement park—Safety in crowds—Strangers in public places—When there aren't any crowds—In case of fire—Staying safe—Glossary—Questions and answers about safety in public places—Helping a friend learn about safety in public places—Did you know?—How to learn more about safety in public places.
  ISBN 1-59296-241-6 (library bound : alk. paper)
  1. Safety education—Juvenile literature. 2. Children and strangers—Juvenile literature.
[1. Safety. 2. Strangers.] I. Title. II. Living well (Child's World (Firm))
  HQ770.7.R22 2005
  613.6'083—dc22   2003027215

TABLE OF CONTENTS

CHAPTER ONE

AT THE
AMUSEMENT PARK

It was a warm summer day, and Matthew was excited. He and his family were spending the day at the amusement park, and he couldn't believe how many rides there were to choose from! He'd already ridden the roller coaster and the carousel. Maybe the Ferris wheel was next.

"Hey, Mom, what about the—"

But Matthew looked around and his mom was not in sight. There were crowds of people around him, but he couldn't see anyone from his family. His dad was wearing a bright yellow baseball cap, but he couldn't spot one nearby. Matthew had just stopped for a minute to look in one shop window. Where could his family have disappeared to so quickly?

*Amusement parks can be a lot of fun! Following a few simple
rules will help you stay safe and have a good time.*

Matthew started to get scared. He didn't recognize anyone around

him. What if his family left without him? "They wouldn't do that," he

reminded himself. "Now think."

Just then he remembered what his dad told him and his sister

when they arrived at the park. He said, "If anyone gets lost, let's all

meet back at this big clock. Right across from the ice-cream stand."

If you get lost at an amusement park, calmly head to the information booth and ask for help.

"OK," Matthew thought.

"Now where was that clock?"

He calmly started walking toward the entrance of the park. He didn't cry or call out for his parents. That would let strangers know he was lost. Then he spotted an information stand, so he walked over to it.

"Hello," he said to the young woman wearing a park uniform.

"Could you tell me where the big clock is? I need to meet my family there." Matthew was a little scared, but he tried not to show it.

"Of course," the woman said with a big smile. "In fact, I'll walk you there myself. My name is Alyssa." She told the other woman behind the counter that she'd be right back.

As they walked toward the clock, Matthew told Alyssa he'd gotten lost. She nodded. "That's what I thought. But you are being very brave about it."

Above the heads in the crowd, they saw the big clock. And there it was—his dad's bright yellow cap. "Matthew!" his mom called. "Thank goodness."

"Yeah," Matthew answered as he ran up to his family. "I guess you guys got lost!" Everybody laughed.

Then Matthew's dad spoke to Alyssa. "Thanks for helping Matthew out."

"No problem. He did the right thing by coming to the

Getting separated from your family in a public place can be frightening. But if you follow some simple safety rules and don't panic, you'll be reunited in no time!

information stand and remembering your meeting place," Alyssa

answered. "Good job, Matthew."

As she walked away, Matthew turned to his mom. "OK, how

about the Ferris wheel next?"

CHAPTER TWO

SAFETY IN CROWDS

There are lots of different kinds of public places. Airports, train stations, and bus stations are public places. So are libraries, museums, zoos, and parks. Usually, public places are busy and full of people. Most of the people in public places are nice, especially the people who work there. But many of the people in public places are strangers, and you need to follow some rules to stay safe.

Whenever you use money in public places, be sure not to show it off. Instead, take out only what you need and return your money to a safe place. A safe place could be a front pocket, a zippered compartment on your belt, or a purse that you wear across your body. You want to be sure that another person

Be sure to keep your money in a safe place where other people can't see it.

would have a hard time getting to your money, so don't carry it in a back pocket or in a purse hung casually over your shoulder.

Be certain to keep your eye on all your belongings. Don't leave a purse or bag sitting on the chair next to you. Keep these items in your lap or at your feet. And if you see bags that have been **abandoned,** tell a trusted adult right away. Such bags could contain **dangerous materials** and

may have been left there on purpose.

Try to stick with your group when you are in a public place.

This means not wandering off to look at something and losing

If you're at an airport and see an abandoned bag, tell an adult as soon as possible. Maybe someone simply forgot it, but it's possible that the luggage could contain dangerous materials.

If you get separated from your group, you can ask a security guard for help.
Talk to your parents about other safe strangers you can trust.

track of where everyone else is. But if you do get lost, don't panic.

If you cry and yell for help, the wrong people may see that you

are by yourself. Instead, ask for help from "safe strangers." These would be people in uniform, such as **security guards** or other workers at the park, museum, or whatever public place you are in.

When you visit a public place such as a mall, talk to the people you are with about a good place to meet up if your group gets spilt up. This meeting place could be an information desk, a store, or one of the exits.

If you don't see anyone like that, other safe strangers are probably women with young children. And when you arrive at any public place, you and your group should always agree on a meeting place in case anyone gets separated.

CHAPTER THREE

STRANGERS IN PUBLIC PLACES

Most of the strangers you see in public places are there for the

same reasons you are—at the zoo to see the animals or at the

airport to fly from one city to another. They don't wish you any

harm, and they are probably good people. If you are with your parents or other adults and a stranger says hi, it is OK to say hi back. He is just being friendly. But if you are by yourself, avoid talking to strangers.

Most strangers are probably just as nice as you are, but it's still important to be cautious around people you don't know.

Some strangers will try to trick you. They might try to **lure** you with candy, money, or even drugs. Run away from any stranger who asks you to come with her or tries to get you into her car. Yell as loudly as you can. You can say, "This is not my mom" or "This is not my dad" to let others know you are in trouble. Find a safe stranger right away and ask for help.

Strangers might even try to lure you with a pet such as this puppy! Don't be fooled, and tell a trusted adult as soon as possible.

Have You Been Fingerprinted?

When you see people on television being finger-printed, they are probably in trouble. These people might have just been arrested for doing something wrong. But being fingerprinted is also a good way to stay safe. Many communities are working with the police to fingerprint children. Having fingerprints on file will help identify children who are lost or need help.

Ask your parents if you have ever been finger-printed. If you haven't, they can check with the local police for details on how to get your finger-prints on file. It is a good idea for your parents to keep recent photos or a video of you on hand. That way, if you are ever lost, they can give the police up-to-date pictures of you. It is also a good idea for your par-ents to keep a current list of all your close friends and their addresses and phone numbers.

CHAPTER FOUR

WHEN THERE AREN'T
ANY CROWDS

rowds of people in public places can be scary. With lots of

people around, it may be hard to keep up with your parents or to

keep an eye on all your belongings. But places without crowds can

be scary, too.

*You might be worried about getting lost in a crowd, but you also need
to be careful in empty places where there aren't many people present.*

Such places are empty parking garages at the mall or lonely trails in a park. Try to avoid places where there aren't other people. Walking through these areas can be dangerous. A stranger could try to kidnap you or take your money, and there might not be anyone around to help you. Always try to stay in areas where there are lots of other people, so you'll be safer if you get separated from your group.

Try to avoid walking alone in an empty parking garage or
any public places where other people aren't present.

When you use a public restroom, it's always wise to have a friend or trusted adult wait for you outside.

Be especially careful when you use public bathrooms. If there are people hanging around who make you uncomfortable, tell your parents or other adults you are with. For extra safety, have a parent or a buddy stand outside the bathroom and wait for you.

CHAPTER FIVE

IN CASE
OF FIRE

You have probably practiced fire drills at school and at home. The same rules apply if there is a fire or other **emergency** in a public place. But there are other rules to remember, too.

If you're in a building and hear a fire alarm sound, calmly head toward the nearest exit.

If someone yells "Fire!" or a fire alarm goes off, don't panic. It is dangerous for lots of people to starting running at once. They can knock other people down and cause **accidents.** Instead, listen to any announcements that are

If you're in a public place when an emergency occurs, instructions may be given over a loudspeaker such as the one shown here.

made and follow any directions that are given to you by the people

who work at the public place.

The most important thing is to get out of the public place as

quickly as possible. If you are outside in a park or zoo, head for the exit. If you are in a large building, follow the fire exits.

Remember, never use an elevator during a fire. Find the stairs

and use those instead. If the building starts filling with smoke,

Always use the stairs to exit a building during a fire.

If there's a fire, the smoke may make it difficult for you to breathe unless you stay close to the ground.

stay low. Smoke rises, so you will be able to breathe better if you

are close to the ground.

Once you are out of the building or the outdoor area, be sure

to stay out. Don't go back for a bag or a camera you left behind.

Your life is more important than those items.

Elevators and Escalators

When you are in public places such as museums and malls, elevators and escalators can get you from one floor to the next. Elevators move straight up and down, connecting one floor with another. Escalators are moving stairs that go up and down at an angle. While these grand inventions may be helpful, they can also be dangerous if you don't follow a few rules.

If you are trying to get on an elevator before the doors close, never block the doorway with bags or your body. The doors may keep closing and you could get stuck. Instead, ask someone to push the Doors Open button, or just wait for the next elevator. Also, never push your way onto a crowded elevator. You could hurt someone—or the elevator could end up carrying too much weight to work correctly.

On an escalator, be considerate of other people. Never push or shove, and always move to the right if someone wishes to walk past you. Take care getting on and off, and always hold the handrail. When you reach the end of the escalator, step away as soon as possible so the people behind you can also step off safely. Don't bring strollers or other wheeled items on escalators. Wheels can get caught on the moving steps. It is best to take these items on elevators instead. And never walk up an escalator while its steps are moving down, or down an escalator while its steps are moving up. Moving against traffic can lead to people getting hurt.

CHAPTER SIX

STAYING SAFE

One good rule for staying safe in a public place is to keep your eyes open. The more you see, the better you will be able to take care of yourself. Make it your **responsibility** to keep safe wherever you are.

If strangers are bothering you or other kids, tell a trusted adult right away. If you see anyone with a weapon, such as a gun or knife, be sure you tell an adult as well.

Public places should be fun places. And you can keep them fun by watching everything around you and staying safe.

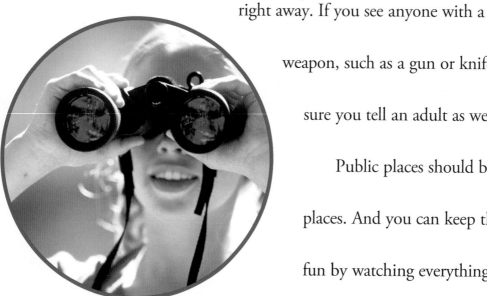

When you're in a public place, always remain observant of what's going on around you.

*Whether you're at a shopping mall, an amusement park, or a beach,
you should enjoy yourself but always remember to stay safe.*

Glossary

abandoned (uh-BAN-dund) Something that is abandoned is empty, deserted, or no longer used.

accidents (AK-si-dunts) Accidents are events that take place unexpectedly and often involve people being hurt.

compartment (kuhm-PART-muhnt) A compartment is a separate area within a container and is used to hold certain things.

dangerous (DAYN-jur-uhss) Something that is dangerous is likely to cause harm. It is not safe.

emergency (i-MUR-juhn-see) An emergency is a sudden and dangerous situation that requires immediate attention.

lure (LOOR) To lure someone is to lead that person into danger.

materials (muh-TIHR-ee-uhlz) Materials are the chemicals or substances that make up something.

responsibility (ri-spon-suh-BIL-uh-tee) A responsibility is a duty or a job.

security guards (si-KYOO-ruh-tee gards) Security guards are people who are hired to watch over a public place and to keep it safe.

Helping a Friend Learn about Safety in Public Places

▸ You and your friend can be safety buddies the next time you go to the mall. Stick together, listen to the adults you are with, and stay away from strangers.

▸ The next time you are at the library, you and your friend can look for all the exit signs. These will tell you how to leave the building in case of a fire or other emergency.

▸ Talk to your friend about times when you have been lost in a public place. Ask her if she has ever been lost. You both can talk about your experiences and decide what you did right in those instances.

Did You Know?

▸ Every day, thousands of children are reported missing. So it is important to keep yourself safe and to let your parents know where you are at all times.

▸ If a stranger grabs you, you should yell as loudly as possible. Kick and hit the stranger. Do anything you can to get away.

▸ People who work in public places are usually eager to help you. If you are in trouble, don't hesitate to ask these people for help.

Questions and Answers about Safety in Public Places

If I am at the mall with my family and I am bored, can I just go to the next store without them? No! You need to stick close to your family, so they know where you are at all times. If you are older, your parents might agree to meet you in another store at an agreed-upon time. But ask permission from your parents before you leave the store you are in.

When I was at the library with my mom, a man asked me if I liked the book I was reading. Was it OK to answer him? If your mom was close by, it was fine to talk to him. Maybe he was trying to pick out a good book for his son or daughter.

At the airport, is it OK to watch bags or luggage for strangers? Absolutely not. Never agree to watch bags for people you do not know. If anyone asks you to do this, tell your parents or an airline worker right away. Many airlines will even make announcements instructing passengers not to watch bags that are not their own.

If I get lost at the zoo, why not just head back to the car? The car is farther away than a spot inside the zoo where you can meet the people you came with. Also, the parking lot or garage where you parked might not be a safe place to wait.

How to Learn More about Safety in Public Places

At the Library

Brown, Marc. *Arthur's Fire Drill.* New York: Random House, 2000.

Chaiet, Donna, and Francine Russell. *The Safe Zone: A Kid's Guide to Personal Safety.* New York: Beech Tree, 1998.

Davis, Meredith. *Up and Away: Taking a Flight.* New York: Mondo, 1997.

Girard, Linda Walvoord. *Who Is a Stranger and What Should I Do?* Morton Grove, Ill.: Albert Whitman, 1985.

Gutman, Bill. *Be Aware of Danger.* New York: Twenty First Century Books, 1997.

Sanders, Pete. *Personal Safety.* Brookfield, Conn.: Millbrook Press, 1998.

On the Web

Visit our home page for lots of links about safety in public places:
http://www.childsworld.com/links.html

Note to Parents, Teachers, and Librarians: We routinely verify our Web links to make sure they're safe, active sites—so encourage your readers to check them out!

Through the Mail or by Phone

Federal Bureau of Investigation
Crimes against Children Program
935 Pennsylvania Avenue NW
Room 11163
Washington, DC 20535
202/324-3666

KlaasKids Foundation
PO Box 925
Sausalito, CA 94966
415/331-6867

National Crime Prevention Council
1000 Connecticut Avenue NW
13th floor
Washington, DC 20036
202/466-6272

National SAFE KIDS Campaign
1301 Pennsylvania Avenue NW
Suite 100
Washington, DC 20004
202/662-0600

Index

About the Author

Lucia Raatma received her bachelor's degree in English literature from the University of South Carolina and her master's degree in cinema studies from New York University. She has written a wide range of books for young people. When she is not researching or writing, she enjoys going to movies, practicing yoga, and spending time with her family. She lives in New York.